WHO TOOK ALL THE PAPER CLIPS?

by → **Rachel Rifat**
CHIC CRAFTER

Fun Things to Do
with Office Supplies
When the Boss
Isn't Looking

RUNNING PRESS
PHILADELPHIA · LONDON

9 8 7 6 5 4 3 2 1

Digit on the right indicates the number of this printing

Library of Congress Control Number: 2008921299

ISBN 978-0-7624-3258-5

Cover and interior design by Jason Kayser

Edited by Diana C. von Glahn

Photos on pages 8–86 by Peter Pawlyschyn

Photos on pages 90–134 by Diana von Glahn and Donna Gambale

Cover photos: © iStockphoto.com/Steve Luker (boss's head); © iStockphoto.com/Oleg Pridhodko (boss's hands); © iStockphoto.com/Jacob Wackerhausen (woman); © iStockphoto.com/Nicholas Sereno (woman's hand); © iStockphoto.com/Christian Ardelean (man's head); © iStockphoto.com/Heidi Kristensen (man's body)

Typography: American Typewriter, Helvetica Rounded, Indoxine, and Serifa

Running Press Book Publishers

2300 Chestnut Street

Philadelphia, PA 19103-4371

Visit us on the web!

www.runningpress.com

This book is dedicated to Mumsy and Rafal.

Mom, thank you for making me "study business first," knowing that the artist in me would always be there. Rafal, thank you for teaching me never to be a disgruntled employee when I can be a creative one instead.

CONTENTS

Introduction

In the corporate environment, there are frequently listless times spent on conference calls or waiting for management to finally approve a project. Instead of becoming disgruntled, become creative! I realized that with the speaker phone on, conferences with the team allowed me to twiddle with paper clips. These paper clips turned into flowers, dogs, and even the Eiffel Tower. Once I completed the Seven Wonders of the World, I moved on to exploratory uses for toilet seat covers.

If you are stuck in a cubicle all day, you may break free from corporate barriers by creating the projects in this book. Detailed step by step instructions and photographic illustrations are included so you can easily function "outside the box."

There are some rules you may want to follow if this is your first time attempting projects at work . . .

1. Never get caught in the supply closet. Simply become best friends with the administrator of the staples.

2. Ensure camouflage for projects by keeping your desk "artistically" messy. This also makes you look like a productive employee.

③ If your boss walks in, simply drop your project into your lap. In the event your boss looks over your shoulder, be prepared by having a clean garbage can in between your knees. Your project can disappear with a simple toss.

④ When displaying your projects, say that your child did it. If you do not have a child, say it was the project of your cube mate's child.

⑤ Always have a lot of books on your desk. If you have a stealth visitor, gently close this book and sandwich it between other books.

⑥ Always keep your office supply receipts handy!

The projects and ideas expressed in this book are meant for recreational purposes only. They are not intended to get you fired, laid off, or demoted. If for some reason you suffer loss of employment, we are not responsible (but we are taking submissions for next year's holiday edition).

Matchstick Incense

When nature calls and the whole office doesn't need to know!

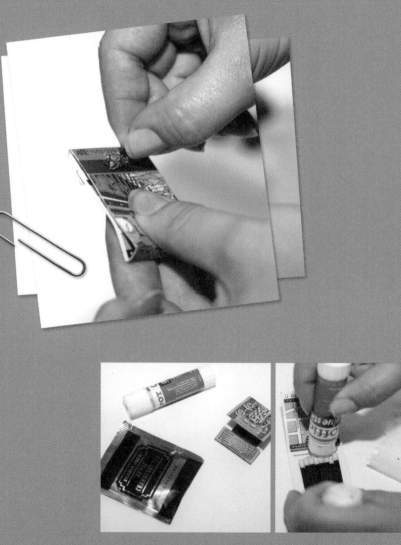

Matchbook

Glue stick

Tea bag, preferably herbal tea

❶ Open the matchbook and glue the front of the match heads with the glue stick.

❷ Tear open the tea bag (hopefully your office has the budget for herbal teas) and spread the fine grains of tea on your desk.

❸ Dip the matchsticks in the tea leaves. Let dry.

❹ To use, strike a match on the non-incensed side, blow it out, and enjoy your moment of Zen.

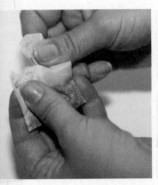 

Anything-But-Boring Bookmark

Who doesn't need something
to take their mind off work?

Paper cutter

8½ x 11-inch overhead transparency

Glue stick

Magazine cut outs, hole punches, mementos

Paper clips

Lighter

❶ Use the paper cutter to cut the transparency into 1½ x 8½-inch strips. You'll use two strips for each bookmark you make.

❷ Glue cut-out images from magazines, hole punches, or other small mementos onto one of the transparency strips. Leave a ⅛-inch margin along the edges of the transparency.

❸ Place another transparency strip on top of the glued images, aligning the edges perfectly. Secure with paper clips.

❹ Quickly run the lit lighter over the edges of the transparencies to seal them—do not go over the paper clips. Carefully remove the paper clips and use the lighter to seal the remaining edges.

Shrinky Finks

Does your boss's heat need downsizing?
Do it with plastic!

MATERIALS:

Scissors

Recycle code 6 plastic (polystyrene):
plates or clear take-out containers

Hole punch

Permanent markers

Aluminum foil

Toaster oven

❶ Cut the plastic to your desired size—expect it to shrink by 75 percent.

❷ If you plan on using your shrinky fink as a key chain or charm, use the hole puncher to cut a hole somewhere in the plastic.

❸ Decorate the plastic with permanent markers. You can also trace a design!

❹ Place the plastic on a sheet of aluminum foil and put it in the toaster oven on low. The plastic shrinks quickly, so be speedy on pulling it out.

Stamp Shop

Personalize your work
with a stamp that screams YOU!

Pen

Square or wedge rubber eraser

Large paper clip or utility knife

Ink pad

❶ Draw a design on the eraser.

❷ Straighten the long end of the paper clip or use the utility knife to carve out your design. Remember, the carved image will print as negative space.

❸ Dab the eraser on the ink pad and stamp away.

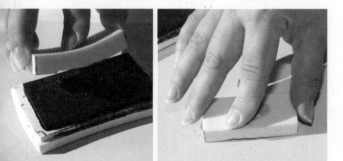

Voodoo Boss

Is your boss making you miserable?
Try this for relief!

Mouse pad

Permanent marker

Card stock

Scissors

Push pins

Glue

❶ Draw the shape of your boss on the mousepad.

❷ Cut the shape out.

❸ Use a permanent marker to write the following ailments on card stock:

- ✕ "migraine"
- ✕ "crotch itch"
- ✕ "carpal tunnel"
- ✕ "toe jam"
- ✕ "back pain"
- ✕ "laryngitis"

❹ Cut the ailments out and glue them to the tops of the push pins. This way you can pick and chose your ailment for the day.

❺ When the mood strikes, place the push pins in select locations.

❻ Order a new mouse pad.

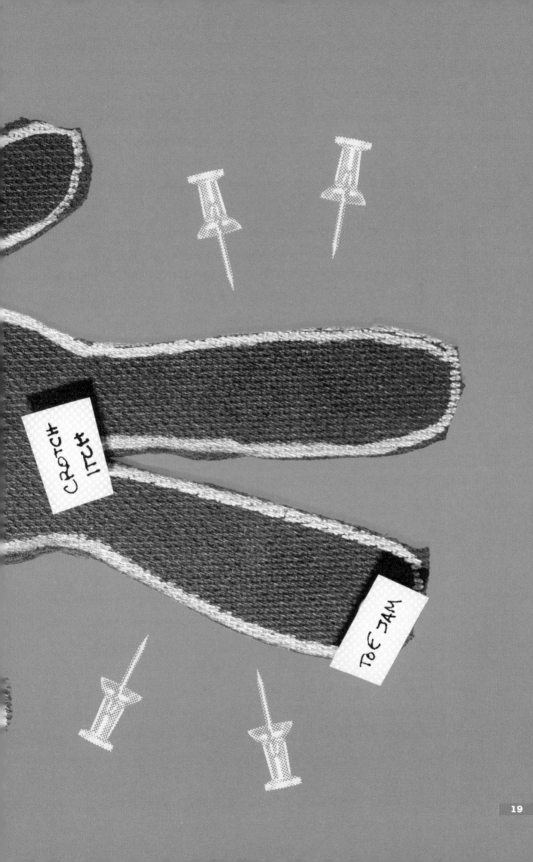

Bitchin' Belt

Keep your pants on in a cinch.

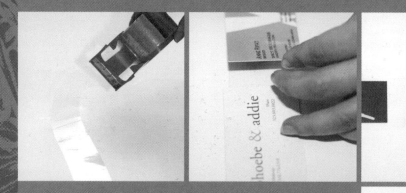

Images, cards, or ticket stubs

Scissors

Packing tape

Lanyard or packing tape

1. Make color photocopies of your favorite images, cards, or ticket stubs (or use the originals). Trim them so they are the width of your packing tape.

2. Lay out one desk length of packing tape, sticky side up.

3. Place the images face down on the tape. Be sure to leave 2 inches at one end without images.

4. For the belt loops, cut the lanyard or packing tape into two 5-inch pieces. If you are using packing tape, fold the lengths of the sticky sides in to make the strips ½ inch wide. Seal the ends to make loops.

5. Wrap the 2-inch end that does not have images around the two loops.

6. Carefully seal the belt with images by placing another length of tape over it.

7. To wear the belt, wrap it around your waist, and stick the tail end through both loops, then bring the end back over the first loop and under the second loop.

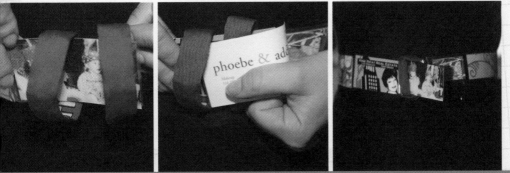

Desktop Greenhouse

Are your plants
always dead?
Get them out of
the asbestos and
into the sun!

Scissors

2 (8.5 x 11) overhead transparencies

Glue

24 wood coffee stirrers

① Cut the transparencies into six 5½ x 4¼-inch pieces.

② Cut 12 of the coffee stirrers to 4¼ inches, and cut the other 12 to 5½ inches.

③ Glue the coffee stirrers horizontally along all sides of the transparencies—place the shorter stirrers along the shorter sides and the longer stirrers along the longer sides of the transparencies. Let dry.

④ Glue together 2 framed transparencies at the corner to make a right angle. Let dry. Add a third and fourth framed transparency to form a rectangle. This will be the sides of your greenhouse. Let dry.

⑤ Glue together the 2 remaining framed transparencies in a 90 degree angle for your roof. Let dry.

⑥ Glue the roof to the sides of your greenhouse. Let dry and place over your plants.

Note: Adjust the size you cut the transparencies to fit your plants.

Mini Desk Shrine

Need a love life?
Make a shrine and pray for one.

Nail file

Mint tin

½ cup vinegar

½ cup bleach

Old nail (look under motivational art)

Plastic cup

Random trinkets and knick knacks

White glue

Clear nail polish, optional

❶ Use the nail file to sand the mint tin and make the surface rough.

❷ Combine the vinegar and bleach in the cup and soak the tin in the mixture overnight. The tin will rust faster if you drop the old nail into the cup, as well.

❸ The next day, dry the rusty tin and use glue to decorate the inside of your tin with trinkets and knick knacks.

❹ Seal your shrine with clear nail polish. For a matte finish, use your fingers to apply white glue—don't worry, it will dry clear.

Mighty Memo Board

Can't get an answer
from IT/HR/AP?
Get your answer
from a direct source!

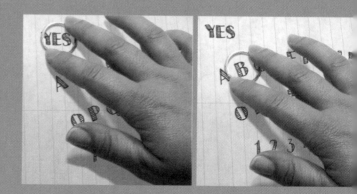

Mighty Memo Board
Ring

❶ Turn the page.

❷ Place the Mighty Memo Board on a flat surface and place a ring on the center of it.

❸ Ask a question of the board, then lightly put two fingers on the ring. Let the ring gently glide over the letters or numbers.

❹ Jot the letters/numbers down at every pause to get your answer.

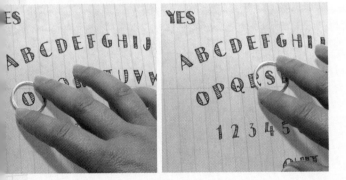

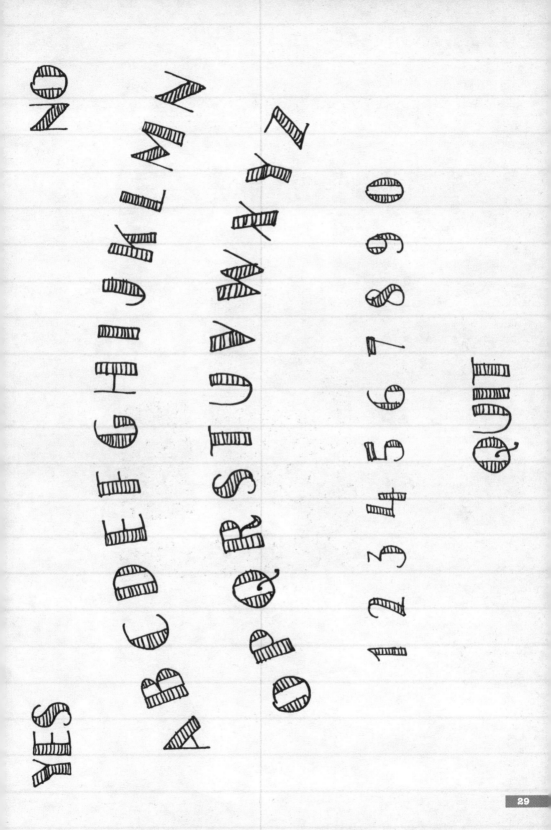

YES NO

A B C D E F G H I J K L M N

O P Q R S T U V W X Y Z

1 2 3 4 5 6 7 8 9 0

QUIT

Coffee Zen Garden

**Find harmony & creativity
through your inner Zen employee.**

2 wood coffee stirrers

Scissors

White glue

Business card box lid

1 pack of coffee

Small statue of deity

❶ Cut a coffee stirrer into four ½-inch pieces.

❷ Evenly space out the ½-inch pieces and add a drop of glue to one end of each.

❸ Carefully place the remaining piece on top of the drops of glue, so that it sits horizontally along the 4 smaller pieces, forming the bottom of a rake. Let dry.

❹ Glue the second coffee stirrer to the center of the bottom of the rake. Let dry,

❺ Pour coffee grounds into the business card lid and level.

❻ Place your deity in the grounds and relax by raking patterns in your garden.

Sticker Factory

Forget that report!
Make something cute,
small, and sticky.

Glue

Photos or images from magazines

Sheet of self-adhesive address or shipping labels

Packing tape

Scissors

❶ Glue the backs of your photos or images clipped from a magazine.

❷ Affix the images to the sheet of labels. Note: The pictures do not have to fit inside the precut lines of the label sheet.

❸ Laminate the sticker sheet by placing clear packing tape over the images. Smooth the sheet out with back of your hand to remove any air bubbles.

❹ Cut out your laminated stickers and decorate the office!

Paper Clip Necklace

These are so coming back in style!

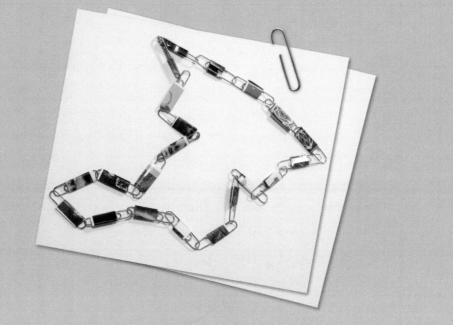

26 paper clips

1 x 1-inch magazine cut outs

Glue stick

Scissors

❶ Connect the paper clips in a circle.

❷ Glue the backs of the cut outs and wrap them around the centers of the paper clips.

❸ Trim off any excess.

❹ Wear!

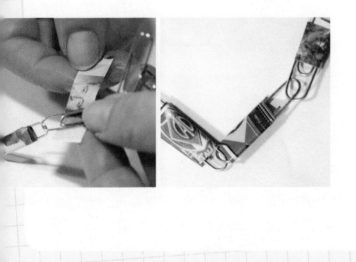

Beaded Curtain

No Door? No Problem!
Make a "beaded" curtain for privacy.

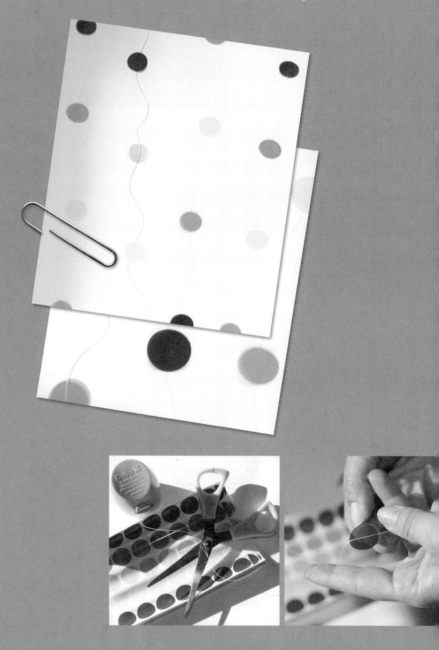

Round color-coding labels,
various colors

Dental floss or string

Tape or push pins

❶ Cut lengths of dental floss to fit the dimensions of the desired curtain.

❷ Affix labels on the string, 2 inches apart, and seal the backs with another label.

❸ Repeat as many times as desired.

❹ Tape or pin the strings up to enclose your space.

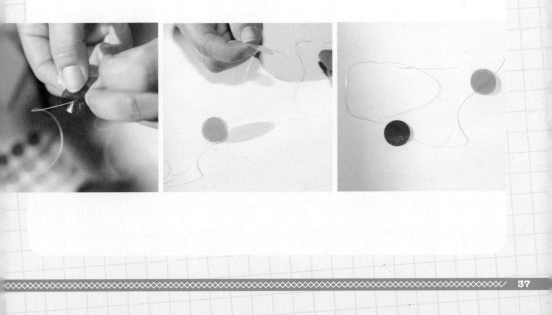

Bad Hair Day?

Fix that frizz with a secret recipe!

Water

Fingertip moistener

① Dampen frizzy hair with water.

② Apply fingertip moistener to your hair sparingly. It is non-toxic, long lasting, and fabulous!

Paper Maché!

The ultimate craft for your cube!

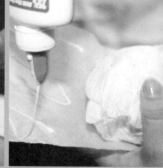

Toilet seat covers

White glue

Masking tape

Markers, nail polish, craft paint

❶ Scrunch up several toilet seat covers to form a ball.

❷ Pour glue all around the ball, then wrap several single sheets of toilet seat covers around the ball.

❸ Repeat and smooth down until your paper maché is the size you want it to be.

❹ Leave it to dry overnight.

❺ Decorate with markers, nail polish, or craft paint.

Desktop Flower Pencils

**Cold and gray outside?
Make your own garden inside!**

Scissors
Colored card stock
Push pin
Pencil with an eraser

❶ Cut out flower petals and leaves from colored card stock in random shapes and colors.

❷ Stack the petals and leaves onto a pushpin in order— remember to put the leaves on last.

❸ Push the pushpin into the center of the pencil eraser.

❹ Bend and crimp the paper to form a pretty flower.

Stress Hand

Need to get a grip?
Try this one on for size.

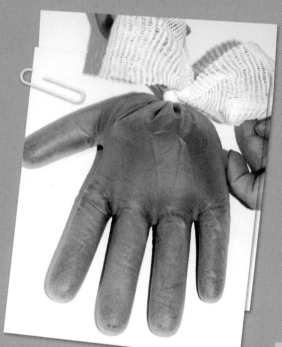

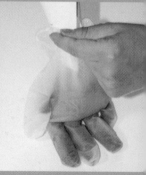

Latex glove

Pack of coffee grounds

Tape

Gauze

1 Fill the glove with coffee grounds.

2 Twist the end and seal it off by wrapping tape around it.

3 Tie the gauze into a bow at the base of the glove.

4 Squeeze your stress away!

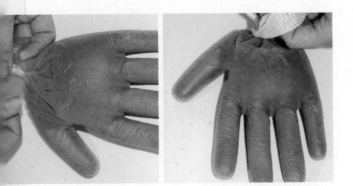

Personalized Keyboard

Forget QWERTY!
Type to your own style.

Letter opener
Computer keyboard
Liquid Wite-Out
Permanent markers
Clear nail polish

1. Use the letter opener to pop out some or all of the keys from your computer keyboard.

2. White out the keys.

3. Use the markers to design new letters or symbols, or create an "eject" button.

4. Apply clear nail polish to coat and seal (test one key—it may smear).

5. Pop the keys back in.

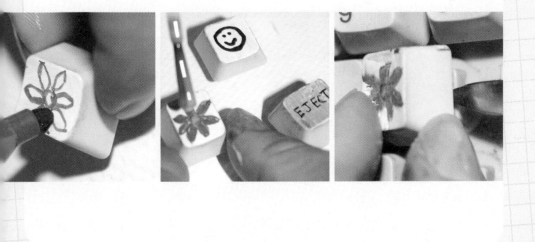

You are a person of imaginative,
yet honest intentions.
07 16 22 29 38, 24

Rubber Band Wish Ball

A magic wish ball
that won't talk back to you.

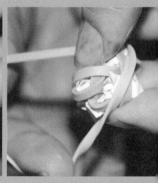

A wish

Piece of paper

A lot of rubber bands

① Write a wish on the piece of paper and wad it up into a ball.

② Tightly wrap a rubber band around the paper ball.

③ Repeat step 2 until you have formed a small rubber band ball.

④ Apply one new rubber band daily until you get your wish.

Matchbox Drawers

Sneaky office mates?
Hide your little secrets in here.

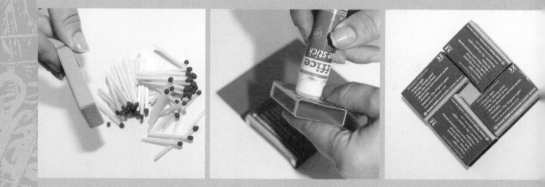

8 small, empty matchboxes

Card stock

Glue

Push pins

① Position four of the matchboxes in a square so you have an opening on each side. Glue the remaining four matchboxes so they sit on top of the first four.

② Place the card stock on top of the boxes and trace the edges of the matchbox square, so you have a square the same size as the boxes. Cut the square out and use it as a guide to cut out another similar square from the second piece of card stock.

③ Glue each piece of card stock to the top and bottom of the matchboxes.

④ Cut out eight 1-inch by ¼-inch strips for the drawer pulls.

⑤ Pull out the matchbox drawers and glue the base of the strips to the bottom of each drawer, making pull-handles.

⑥ Place the drawers back in the boxes and hide your secrets!

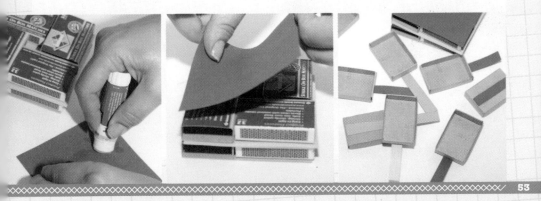

Reupholstered Bubble Chair

Put a little bounce in your butt!

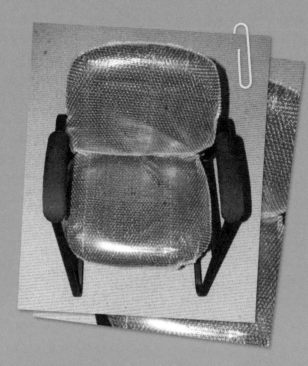

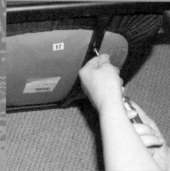

Screwdriver

Upholstered chair

Bubble wrap

Stapler

Scissors

❶ Unscrew the seat of the chair.

❷ Cut a piece of bubble wrap so that it is 2 inches larger on all sides than the seat cushion.

❸ Wrap the bubble wrap around the seat and staple the back at opposing corners—gather the other two corners and staple.

❹ Smooth the bubble wrap at the edges and staple, always working from one side to the next.

❺ Cut off any excess bubble wrap.

❻ Repeat instructions for the back of the chair.

❼ Screw the chair back together and bounce away.

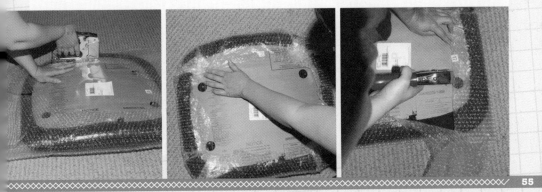

Bubble Pillow

Give that back a break.

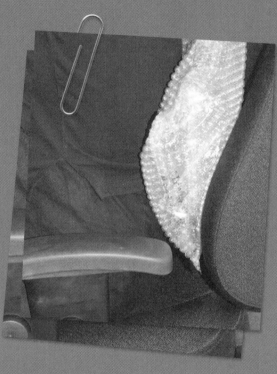

Bubble wrap

Inflated bubble bag

Packing tape

❶ Wrap bubble wrap around the bubble bag.

❷ Seal with tape.

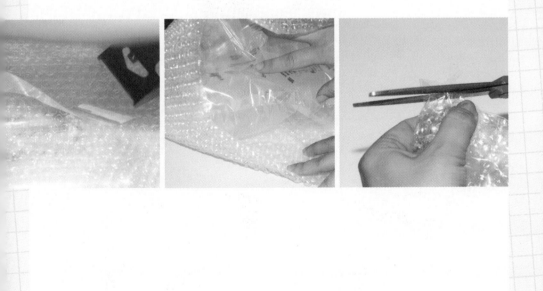

Hole Punched Frame

Punch up your office décor with framed family photos.

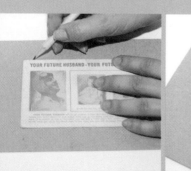

8½ x 11 memo pad cardboard, cut in half

Photos of loved ones

Ruler

Scissors

Glue stick

Hole punches

Transparency

Binder clip

❶ Place a photo in the center of one of the cardboards and trace around the picture.

❷ Use the ruler to measure a ¼-inch margin inside of the traced outline; cut out the smaller center square.

❸ Trace the shape of the frame onto the transparency, cut it to size, and glue it to the back of the frame.

❹ Glue the top corners of the frame and adhere to the second piece of cardboard.

❺ Glue the face of the frame and sprinkle hole punches over the glue. Press them to stick and let dry.

❻ Place the picture in the frame, attach a binder clip to the bottom, and remove the wires from the clip. Stand the frame on your desk.

Pretty Pencils

Put a little pizzazz on your pencils!

Glue stick

¼ x 8-inch piece of decorative paper

Pencil

Scissors

① Glue the back of the paper and wrap it tightly around the pencil so it ends just below the metal head.

② Cut off any excess at the tip of the pencil.

③ Roll the wrapped pencil back and forth to get a tighter seal.

④ Let the glue dry—you may want to use binder clips to hold your seam together.

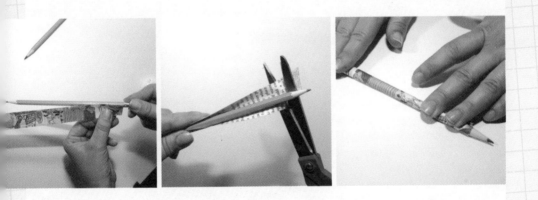

Pen Gun

Take good care of an archenemy!

Ballpoint pen that can be disassembled

Small pieces of paper

1. Remove the ink cartridge from the pen.
2. Chew on a piece of paper to make a spit wad.
3. Insert the wad into the barrel of the pen.
4. Blow at unwilling subject.
5. Repeat as necessary.

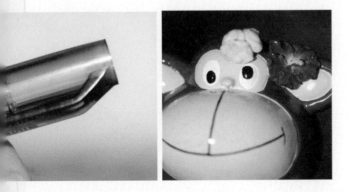

Family Theatre

Why go home when you
can play with the family at work?

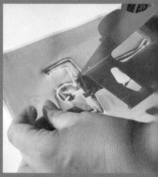

Glue

Photocopied photos of family members

Foam board

Clear packing tape

Craft knife

Coffee stirrers

1. Glue the photographs to the foam board.

2. Laminate the photos by sealing with clear packing tape.

3. Trim the edges with the craft knife.

4. Glue the cut-out to the coffee stirrer to make a puppet.

5. Play!

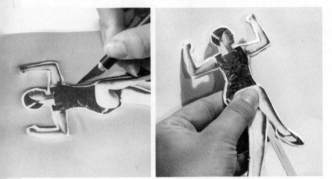

Ransom Clock

Do you feel like a hostage at work?
Take over the clock!

Clock

Paper clip

Numbers cut out from magazines

① Remove the plastic face from the clock by popping it out from the back using a bent paper clip.

② Remove the hands (remember the stacking order).

③ Glue the numbers to cover the clock's original numbers (my favorite is to use only 5's).

④ Replace the hands and plastic face.

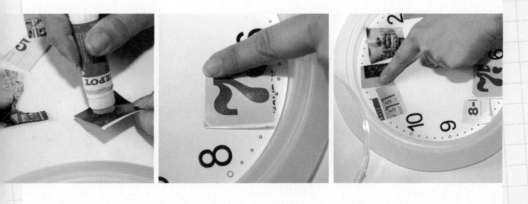

Monitor
Mirror Mosaic

Put those burnt discs to use!

Eyeglasses, for protection

Scissors

CDs

Computer monitor

White glue

❶ Put on the glasses to protect your eyes.

❷ Use scissors to cut the CDs into different shaped pieces.
Be careful, as they sometimes shatter.

❸ Glue the pieces to the frame of your computer monitor so
that the reflective part of the CD pieces shows. Fill in any
empty patches with smaller cut sizes.

Note: You can also use the printed side for a colored mosaic.

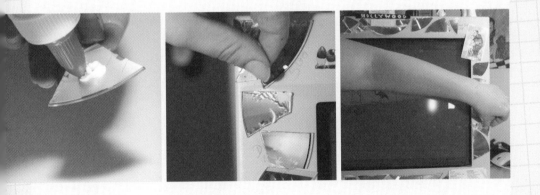

Paper Tops

Take a spin in the office

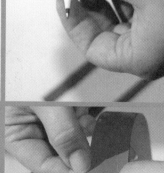

MATERIALS:

Colored paper

Scissors

Empty ballpoint pen cartridge

Glue stick or white glue

1. Cut the paper into strips that are 1-, ¾-, ½-, and ¼-inch-wide.

2. Glue the back of the 1-inch strip and tightly wrap it around the base of the cartridge.

3. Glue the back of the ¾-inch strip and tightly wrap it around the top of the 1-inch piece. Repeat with the ½-inch and ¼-inch pieces.

4. Trim off the end of the cartridge, leaving a 1-inch stem.

5. Spin.

Note: This project is difficult and may require additional strips of paper to get the top to spin.

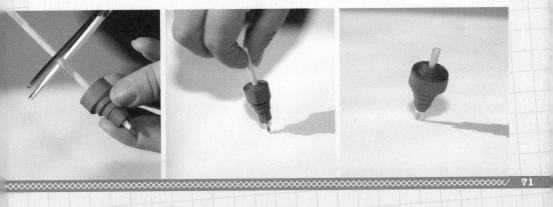

Japanese Stab Bound Book

Write your Zen down.

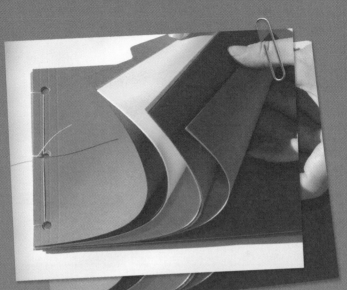

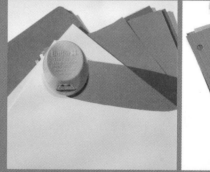

1 colored file folder

20 sheets of paper

Hole puncher

Pencil

Dental floss

❶ Cut the folder and paper into 5½ x 8½-inch strips.

❷ Punch three holes along the 5½-inch side of the folder strips.

❸ Punch three holes in the sheets of paper to match.

❹ Keeping the margins with the holes on the left side, sandwich the paper between the two strips of the cut folder. With a pencil, lightly mark your holes #1, #2, and #3. This will be erased at the end of the project.

❺ Thread the dental floss down through the hole #2 leaving a 4-inch tail.

(continued)

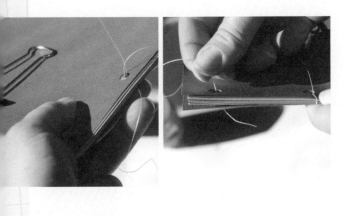

⑥ With your thumb on the tail, use your other hand and bring the floss around the side and down hole #2 again. Always keep the floss tight.

⑦ Bring the floss up hole #1, wrap it around, and pull the floss back up hole #1.

⑧ Thread the floss down hole #2, wrap it around the left side, and thread the floss back down hole #2.

⑨ Bring the floss up hole #3, wrap it around the left side, and pull the floss back up hole #3.

⑩ Thread it down hole #2 and tie tightly with the tail in a double-knot.

⑪ Cut off any excess and erase the numbered marks.

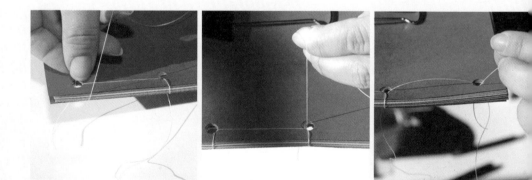

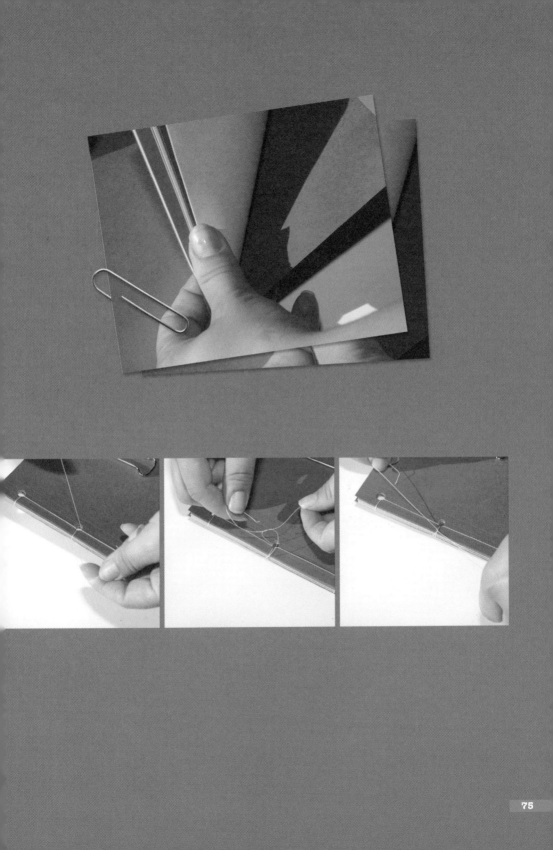

Painted Walls

Paint those nasty sanitarium walls
with removable paint!

Colored chalk

Sheet of paper

Cup

Water

Scissors

Sponge

❶ Pulverize the chalk over the piece of paper.

❷ Carefully create a funnel out of the paper and transfer the chalk to the cup.

❸ To create paint, add a little water to the chalk and mix.

❹ Cut the sponge into shapes, dip it into the paint, and dab along your walls.

Book Safe

Hide your stash
where no one will ever look.

Glue stick

Large reference book

Binder clips

Craft knife

❶ Glue each page together from the back of the book to page 15.

❷ Clamp the glued pages and back cover with binder clips.

❸ Draw a rectangle on page 15 (it should be on the right hand side) leaving a ½-inch margin on all sides.

❹ Use the craft knife to cut a square, following the guide you just drew; cut through the pages, leaving some of the last pages intact.

❺ Hollow out the pages and use the space to stealthily store your valuables.

Scratch 'n Sniff Memo Pad

Spend time smelling, not staring, at those boring meetings!

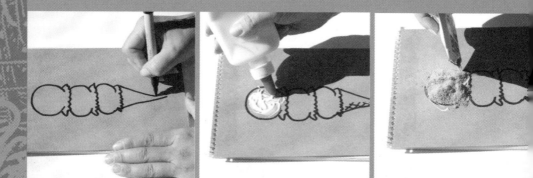

Cardboard from a memo pad

Flavored drink powders, powdered
hot chocolate, coffee creamer,
lemonade, coffee

White glue

1 Draw a shape on the cardboard that you want to make
into a scratch 'n sniff.

2 Glue the area for the first scent.

3 Pour the flavored powder onto the glue.

4 Shake off any excess.

5 Repeat steps 2 through 4 until you have completed your
scratch 'n sniff heaven.

Transparency Stencil

Make your mark.

Permanent marker

Transparency

Craft knife

Stamp pad

Sponge

❶ Use the permanent marker to trace an image onto the transparency.

❷ Use the craft knife to cut out the image.

❸ Tape the stencil down to where you want to make your mark.

❹ Sponge stamp pad ink onto your stencil.

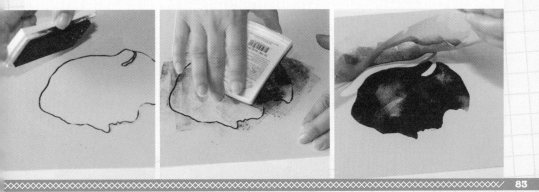

Glue Necklace

A lacy masterpiece!

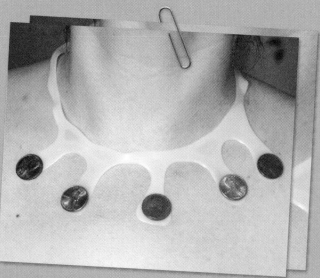

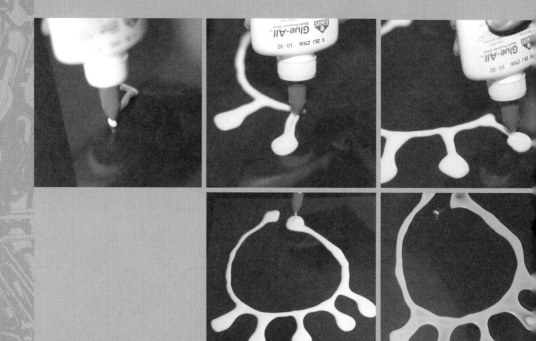

White glue

Transparency

Coins or other treasures, optional

Hole puncher

Brass brads

1. Pour the glue onto the transparency, forming an open, necklace-sized circle.

2. Add drops of glue along the circle to create a tear drop effect. Add nickel-sized glue drops to the ends of the necklace. Add coins or other treasures, if desired.

3. Let dry overnight.

4. Carefully peel the necklace off of the transparency.

5. Punch holes in the ends of the necklace and attach them with the brass fastener.

6. Show off your new necklace.

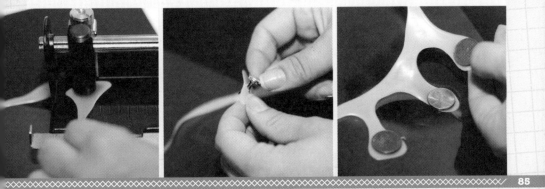

Business Card Clear Purse

So the boss knows you
are not stealing office supplies.

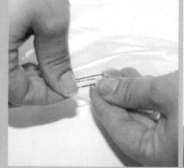

2 business card sheet protectors

Paper clips

Matches/Lighter

Cards, images, trinkets, etc.

1. Line up the sheet protectors so the slot openings face each other; carefully cut off the strips that have the binder holes and reserve.

2. Secure the transparencies with paperclips and seal the edges—with the exception of the cut side—by running a lit match or lighter along them, melting the plastic together.

3. Glue the strips with the binder holes and secure to each other so that the holes are aligned.

4. Run a lit match or lighter along the top left and right corners of the purse, and attach the glued strip, making a purse strap.

5. Fill the sheet protectors with cards, images, trinkets, or clippings. The decorative side should face the opposite slot openings.

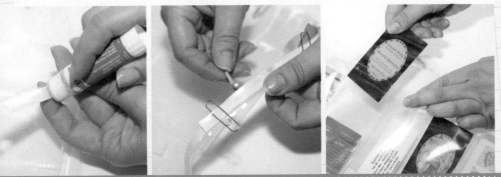

Inter Office Communication

Communicate secretly to your cubicle mate.

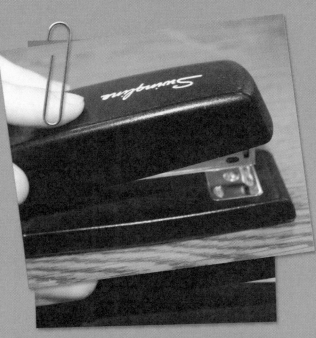

Morse code (see next page)

Stapler

❶ Practice Morse code daily by tapping on your stapler. The dots represent quick taps and the dashes are long taps.

❷ Send secret messages to your workmate.

Useful codes:

Break
▬ • • •   • ▬ •   •   • ▬ ▬   ▬ • ▬

Boss Coming
▬ • • •   ▬ ▬ ▬   • • •   • • •
▬ • ▬ •   • ▬ ▬ ▬   ▬ ▬ ▬   • •   ▬ • ▬   ▬ ▬ •

Go Home
▬ ▬ •   ▬ ▬ ▬
• • • •   ▬ ▬ ▬   •

SOS
• • •   ▬ ▬ ▬   • • •

Hide
• • • •   • •   ▬ • •   •

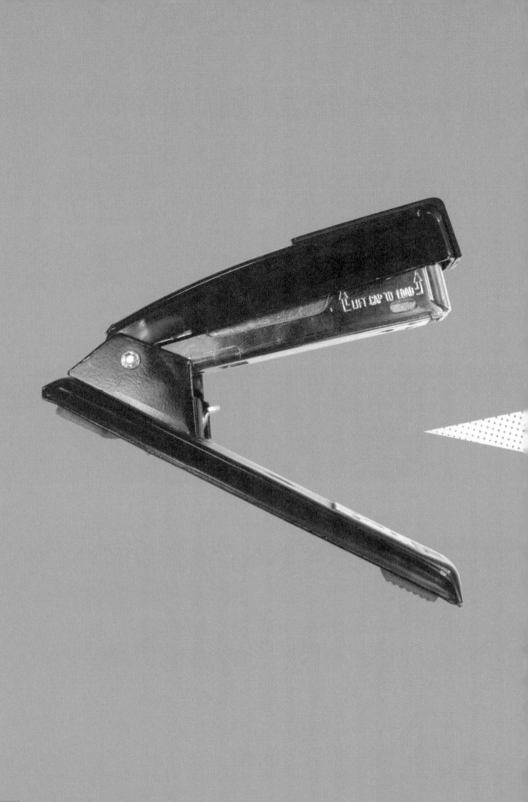

Post-It
Marilyn Mural

Tired of motivational posters?
Make some pop art!

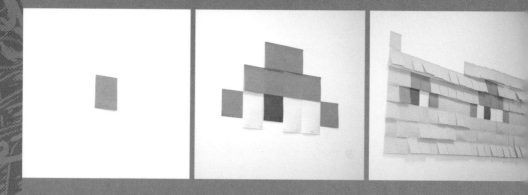

7½ square foot wall (avoid sunny spaces, as the post-its will fade)

3 x 3 Post-It notes (use 2 x 2 notes for a 5-square-foot space) in the following colors:

- × 299 yellow – hair
- × 303 pink – face
- × 13 fuchsia – lips
- × 14 green – earrings
- × 12 blue – eye shadow
- × 3 black or purple – eyes and mole
- × 4 white – white of the eyes

❶ Find the center point of the wall and place the first post-it in blue (see "x" on diagram – Marilyn's eye shadow).

❷ Follow the diagram matching it to the corresponding colored post-it.

❸ Line up all of the edges of the notes against each other so the image does not skew. Chalk may be used to draw horizontal guidelines.

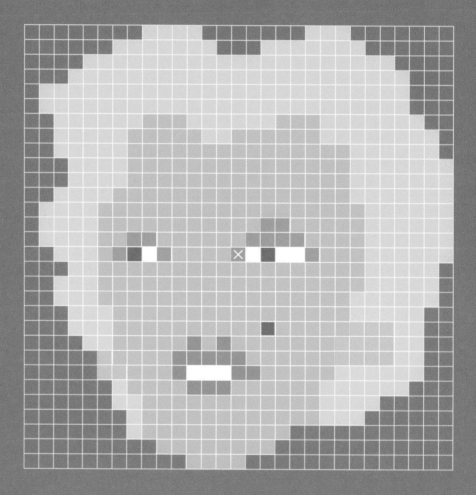

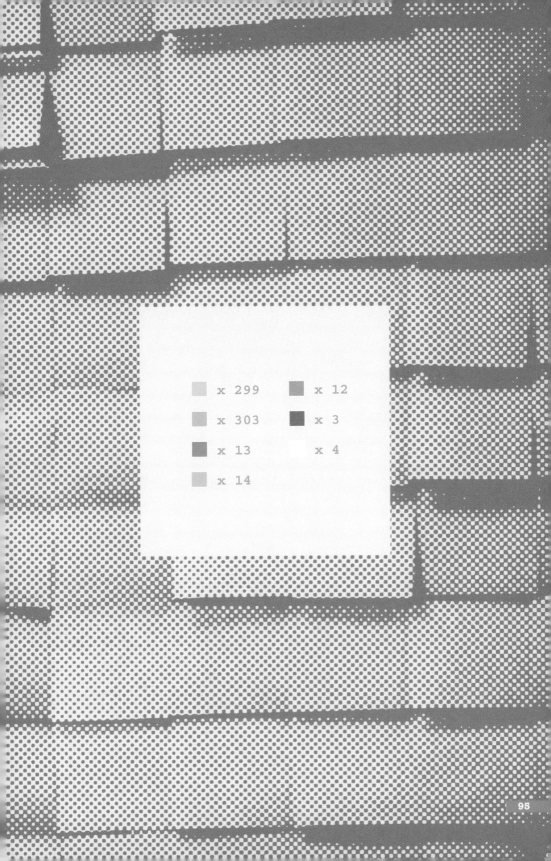

■ x 299   ■ x 12

■ x 303   ■ x 3

■ x 13   x 4

■ x 14

Marble Paper

For the connoisseur of fine paper.

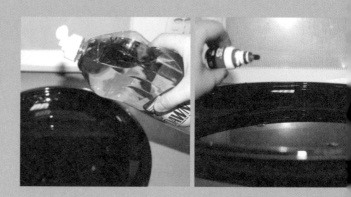

MATERIALS:

Large plastic food container

Water

Dishwashing liquid

Ink

Toothpick

Heavy paper

❶ Fill half of the plastic container with water, then add a few drops of dishwashing liquid.

❷ Gently add drops of the ink to the surface of the water.

❸ To create patterns, use the toothpick to trail the ink in the water.

❹ Gently place the paper on the surface of the water.

❺ Wait 2 seconds, then peel the paper from the water.

❻ Set the paper aside to dry.

Office Mate Dart Board

Relieve stress without having to go postal.

Scissors

White glue or glue stick

Ceiling tile or cork board

Digital camera or pictures from a
magazine (optional)

Permanent marker

❶ Copy the image of the dartboard on the following page,
increasing the size as big as you'd like; cut out the circular
board.

❷ Glue the dartboard image to a ceiling tile or cork board.

❸ Photograph your office mates, print out the pictures, and
glue in strategic places to the dartboard or use cut out
images from a magazine.

❹ Use the darts from the next project to play.

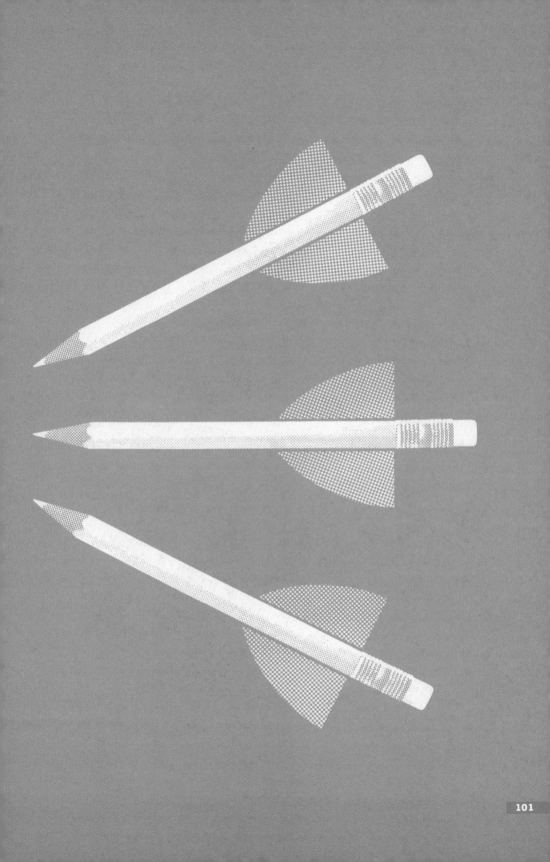

Pencil Darts

Dare to make a small, narrow, pointed missile.

3 pencils

Pencil sharpener

Packing tape

Card stock

Scissors

❶ Sharpen the pencils to three-fourths their original size, about 2 inches.

❷ Cut the cardstock into three triangles measuring 1 inch x .5 inch x 1.5 inches (see image below). Make sure the 1.5 inch side is rounded.

❸ Wrap tape around each triangle.

❹ Attach the triangles to the end of the pencil with packing tape.

Yellow or White Pages Paper Vase

Make a gorgeous paper sculpture for a single bud.

Yellow or White Pages

White glue

Paper towel tube

Paper

❶ Fold the top right of the first page of the Yellow or White Pages down into the binding.

❷ Fold it again from the right edge into the binding.

❸ Repeat this process for each page until all the pages have been folded into the binding. If it gets difficult to fold, bend the binding back to give more leeway.

❹ Glue the front and the back cover together. The pages should form a perfect circle.

❺ Cut the excess of the cover and backs to match the folded page size.

❻ Cut the paper towel tube lengthwise and insert the cut tube, in the center of the vase, for support.

❼ Wad up a small ball of paper and stuff down the tube about four inches to halt your flower from hitting the bottom.

❽ Fluff up your pages and insert a single rose or a pencil top flower.

Family Memories Bracelet

**Charm your wrist
with some family photos.**

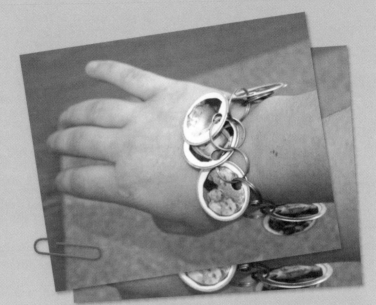

6 key tags

Permanent marker

Pictures

Scissors

Glue stick

Hole punch

1. Remove the rings from the key tags.

2. Using one of the key tags as a guide, trace the inner circle onto family pictures.

3. Cut out the images and paste them onto the key tags.

4. Hole punch where the existing hole is on the tag.

5. Replace the rings on the key tags, and hook them together to form a bracelet.

Terra Firma Terrarium

Scrap the discs and make
an eco garden in your office.

Plastic CD spindle container of
100 CD's or more

10 pen caps

Potting dirt

Plant clippings or fruit seeds

Small figurines (optional)

1. Wash out the CD tower and turn it upside down. Remove the spindle from the bottom.

2. Drop the pen caps randomly into the bottom. These will serve as drainage.

3. Add 5 inches of dirt and some water to moisten it.

4. Add the plant clippings and space them out so they have room to grow.

5. Place decorative elements in the terrarium. Toys from children's meals or other figures may be used.

6. Put the base of the CD tower on the tower and close.

7. Lightly water the plant every few months, only when the dirt begins to dry. The dirt should always be moist. If it is over-watered the plants will not survive.

8. Place in indirect sunlight.

Rockin' Ruler Cuff

Fashion according to a "ruleR".

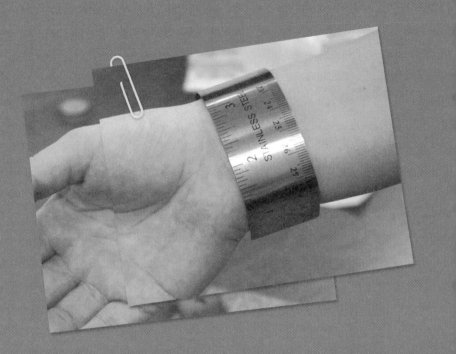

Utility knife

Metal ruler

Nail file

1. Making strong and slow cuts with the utility knife, cut the metal ruler at the 6-inch mark.

2. File around the cut edges to remove sharp points.

3. Bend the ruler gently in the middle and keep bending it to make an oval shape.

4. Slip on the cuff, wear, and rock out.

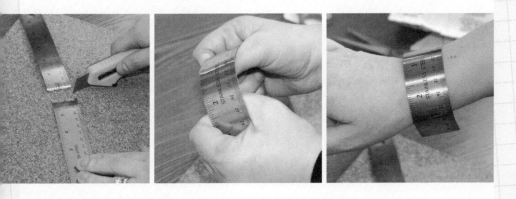

Hot Knife Cuff

The cutting edge accessory
at the office.

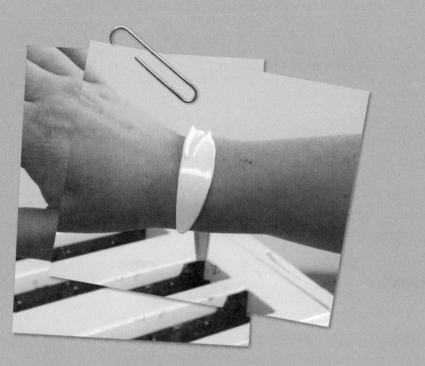

Toaster

Plastic knife

Scissors

❶ Turn an upright toaster on.

❷ Hold the knife over the hot opening with a pair of scissors.

❸ When the knife becomes malleable, bend it into a circle.

❹ Let the knife cool then slip it on.

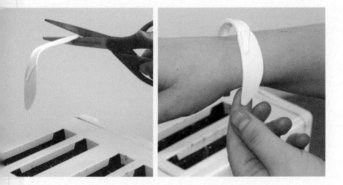

Cardboard
Chandelier

When fluorescent lighting
just won't do.

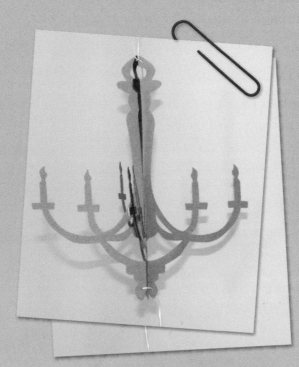

Cardboard box

Chandelier template (on next page)

Scissors or utility knife

Dental floss or string

① Enlarge and photocopy the chandelier template on the next page to the size of your cardboard box.

② Trace and cut the chandelier template onto your box.

③ Cut out all solid lines.

④ Interlock both pieces by sliding the top chandelier over the bottom chandelier,

⑤ Loop bottom holes with dental floss to secure the chandelier.

⑥ Loop dental floss through the top holes and hang.

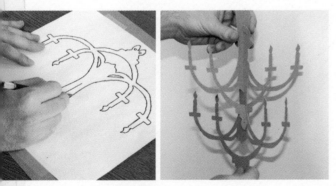

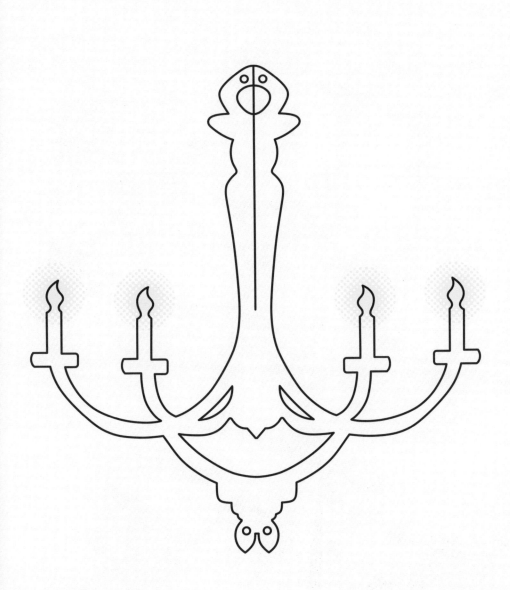

Computer Monitor Piñata

Have a fiesta!

Permanent marker

Letterhead box

Scissors

Packing tape

Rope or string

Yellow and blue Post-It notes

12-inch wooden ruler

➊ Draw a rounded rectangle onto the letterbox, leaving a 2-inch margin on all sides.

➋ Cut a hole in the bottom of the box that is big enough to allow your hand to fit through the hole. Seal the insides of the box with packing tape (post-it's will not stick to packing tape). Keep the cut portion open to allow you to fill the piñata with goodies.

➌ Poke two small holes at the top of the box and attach the rope to hang the piñata.

➍ Tightly roll a single blue post-it and cut it into eight strips, leaving the sticky part in tact.

(continued)

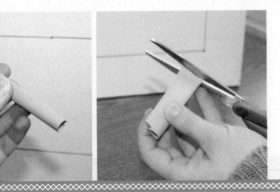

⑤ Attach the sticky part to the face of the monitor (the rounded rectangle) and repeat until the monitor is completely filled in. Fluff up the curls of the strips.

⑥ Repeat instructions four and five to cover the frame of the monitor with yellow post-it notes.

⑦ Fill the piñata with candy and office supplies. Seal the hole with packing tape.

⑧ Hang the piñata.

⑨ Blindfold a coworker and have him or her whack the piñata with the ruler.

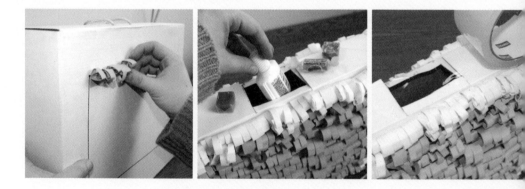

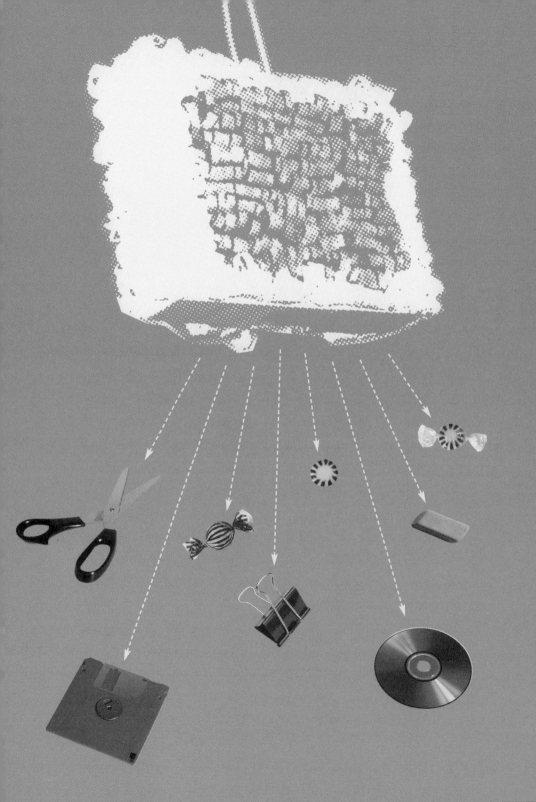

Paint-by-Numbers Mona Lisa

Turn that frown upside down
and enjoy the scent of coffee paint.

Coffee bag

Coffee filter

Dental floss or string

6 coffee cups

Heavy bond paper

Paintbrush

❶ Place the coffee in a coffee filter. Tie the filter closed with floss.

❷ Put the filter in a coffee cup and fill with boiling water. Let it steep until the coffee is very dark. Remove the filter. Label the cup #6.

❸ Divide the coffee evenly into the remaining coffee cups and number them 1 to 5.

❹ Add 5 tablespoons of water to coffee cup #1; 4 tablespoons of water to coffee cup #2; 3 tablespoons of water to coffee cup #3; 2 tablespoons of water to coffee cup #4; and 1 tablespoon of water to coffee cup #5. Adjustments may be needed to get color differentiation.

(continued)

⑤ Copy the image of the Mona Lisa without the numbers onto the paper.

⑥ Following the numbered version of the Mona Lisa, use the corresponding numbers on the coffee cups to paint. (If the numbers are too hard to read, make an enlarged copy of the numbered Mona.)

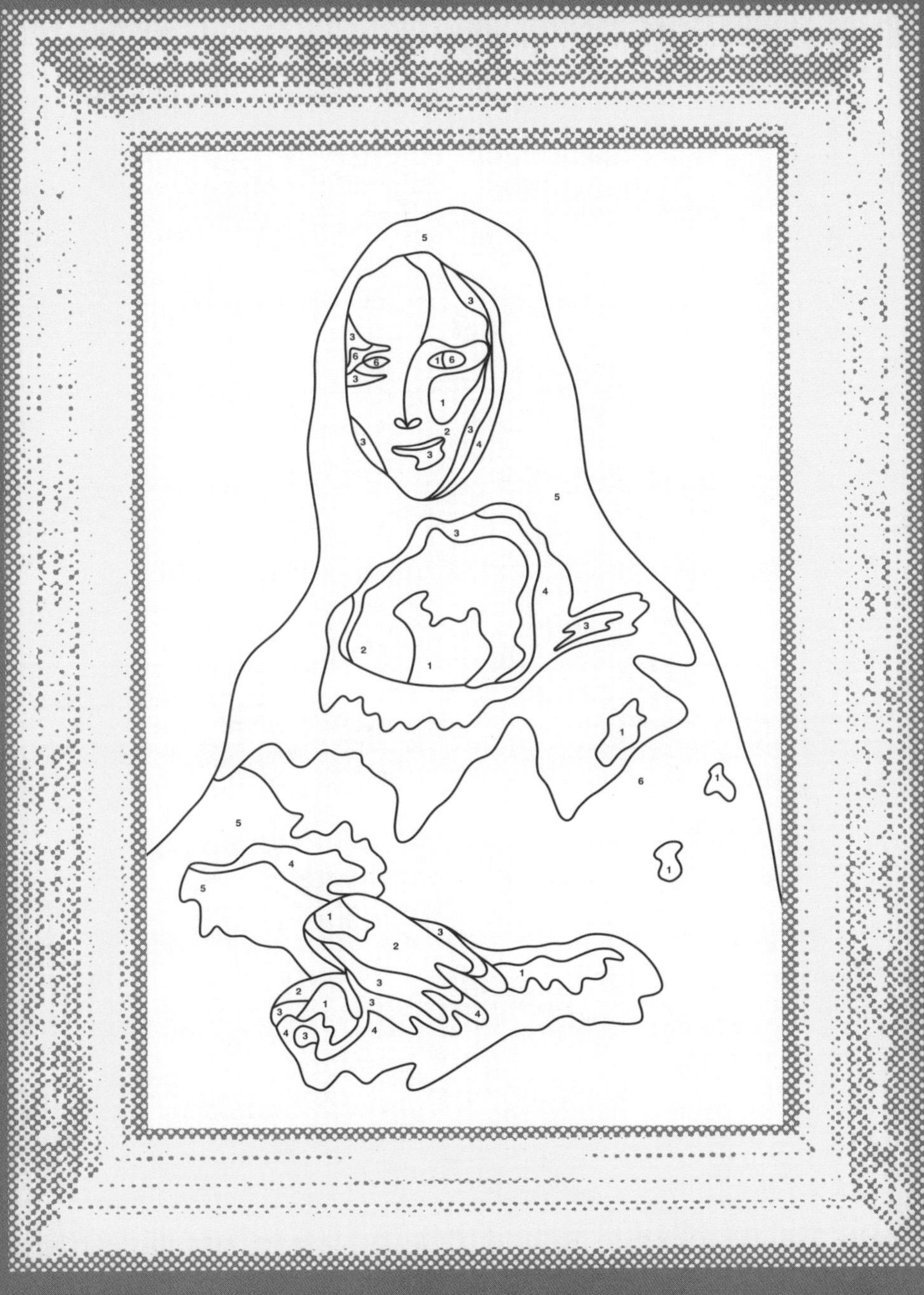

Go Fish Game

Fish for a golden parachute
or mental leave!

Dental floss or string

Chopsticks

Strong magnet

Packing tape

Glue stick

Foam core

Utility knife

Large paper clips

CD tower

Blue paper

Scissors

❶ Make a fishing rod by tying 1 foot of dental floss around the pointy end of a chopstick.

❷ At the other end of the floss, attach the magnet with the tape.

❸ Copy the diagram on page 129.

❹ Glue the diagram to a 6 x 9 piece of foam core.

❺ Cut around the solid lines of the images.

(continued)

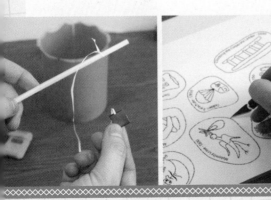

6 Tape the paper clips to the backs of the images. Make sure the paper clips are sticking out at one end so they are attracted by the magnet of the fishing rod.

7 Create a tank by turning an empty CD tower upside down and lining it with blue paper. Cut the top of the paper in wave form for an ocean effect.

8 Place your go fish pieces in the CD tower.

9 Make another fishing rod for a colleague and take turns catching fish.

10 The one with the most cash at the end of the game wins.

Jury Duty $300

Gift Cart $100

Moonlighting $500

Mental Leave $400

Team Player $200

Maternity Leave $800

Golden Parachute $900

Early Retirement $1,000

Head Hunter Job $700

Climbing the Corporate Ladder $600

Ringleader

Cheap gift card from the boss?
Turn it into a fabulous ring
to wear on your finger!

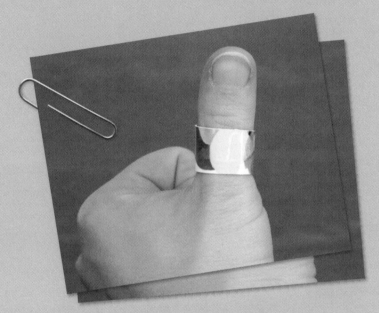

Gift card

Scissors

Toaster

Highlighter cap

1. Cut the gift card into a .5 x 2.25-inch strip (this will be the design of your ring)

2. Use scissors to hold the strip over a hot toaster.

3. When the card begins to turn limp, immediately wrap it around the highlighter cap.

4. Wait for it to cool, then wear.

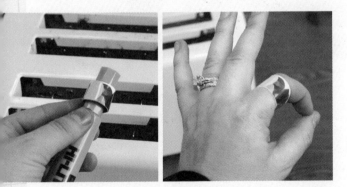

Corporate
Ladder Discs

Why are you waiting to climb
the corporate ladder, when you
can just sit back and play
with your personal ladder?!

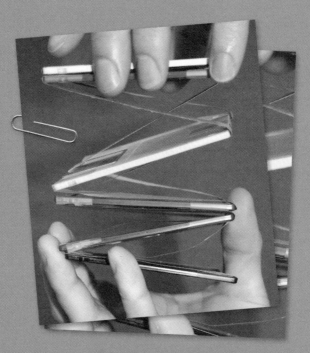

Colored construction paper

Scissors

6 computer floppy disks

Packing tape

❶ Cut the paper into 15 strips that are ½ inch wide and 6 inches long.

❷ Stack the floppy disks. Mentally label them 1 through 6, with 1 being the top disk.

❸ On the bottom center of disk number 1, tape the top 1 inch of a strip of paper.

❹ Wrap the strip beneath disk 1 and over the top of disk 2. Tape the end beneath the center of disk 2.

❺ Repeat instructions 3 to 4 for the rest of the disks so that disk 2 links to disk 3, disk 3 to disk 4, and so forth.

(continued)

⑥ Still keeping the disks in order, take 2 strips and tape the bottom 1 inch to the top left and right edges of disk 1.

⑦ Wrap the strips under disk 1 and over the bottom of disk 2. Tape the ends beneath the right and left edges of disk 2.

⑧ Repeat instructions 6 to 7 for the rest of the disks. Don't be afraid to flip the disks to get the best taping angle!

⑨ Play by holding the top disk and folding it to the second disk.

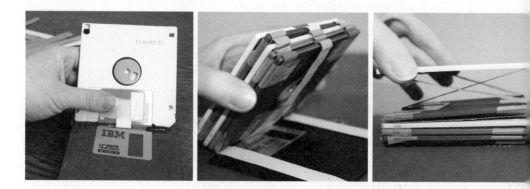

Rachel Rifat worked the Southern California corporate life where she became captivated by politics, hypocrisy, and Little Man Syndrome. She packed her bags to study international business in China when she decided she could not stand to see another manager wearing a Hawaiian shirt and shorts at a beer bust.

After escaping the chaos of Beijing's democracy movement in 1989, she landed in Cairo to pursue other ventures. While living in Egypt, she witnessed riots during Desert Storm and decided to head back to the good old U.S.A. She moved to Hollywood, where she opened Hollywood Dog, a fortune cookie company for dogs. In 1999, she was named Los Angeles Business Woman of the Year. She has been published and written about in *The Wall Street Journal*, *People Magazine*, *Entrepreneur Magazine*, and *The Los Angeles Times*.

Rachel lives in Hollywood with her husband Michael, Stanley their greyhound, and a house full of projects in progress (including the house). In addition to writing, she is a graphic designer, an illustrator, an exhibiting artist, and a chocolate blogger (chocolate-snob.com). This is her first book.

ACKNOWLEDGEMENTS

A very special thank you goes out to my friend, Peter Pawlyschyn. You are an amazing photographer and I cannot thank you enough for taking photos and providing art direction on those hot weekends without AC.

Much gratitude goes to the ever talented Taryn Fagerness at the Sandra Dijkstra Literary Agency, my forgiving editor Diana von Glahn at Running Press, and the fabulous designer Jason Kayser.

Appreciation goes to Marci Goot from National Lampoon, Harry Youtt, Bronwyn and Roberto Hamilton for being mentors and providing me with fantastic leads.

Thank you to my friends and family for their undying support of my crazy ideas. . . . Rafal Staros, Dean Leventini, Evelyne Hochstrasser, Laura Condra, Dayna West at Buffalo Productions, Bobby Moffett, Tom Thompson, Allan "Dino" Murray, Pascal Colrat, Billie Murphy, Margaret Fitzsimons Daniella Peters, Christian Arroyo, my boss John Hinrichs, Anne Rifat (a.k.a. Mumsy) and my twin, Matthew Rifat.

Of course, nothing would have ever been possible without Martha Stewart for making crafting elegant and Rosie O'Donnell for making crafts accessible.